BEFORE I LEAVE CANADA

A poetry collection

by

C. D. Melley

BEFORE I LEAVE CANADA

C. D. Melley

Before I Leave Canada
Copyright © 2015 by C. D. Melley

Published by Douglas J. McLeod

Cover Photo: Douglas J. McLeod
First Paperback Edition: 2015

ISBN: 978-0993773242
ISBN-10: 0993773249

10 9 8 7 6 5 4 3 2 1

For my darling Catherine,

We're in this together, forever.

Other poetry collections by C. D. Melley

Slammin' on the Rails

Poems For a Winter's Night

Flavour Dilemma

Anyone who knows me
Knows I am loyal to a certain brand
Of coffee shops named for a hockey player
With locations spanning across the land.

Their bakery items are divine
So much so, I have named my pup after their doughnut holes
But, it is their coffee that makes them famous
People wish the cups were the size of bowls.

However, I am in a rival company's locale
As I write this bit of prose
Sipping on a cool creation
The barista crafted for my palette.

I am at a loss for my loyalty
Betraying my country for enjoyment
Iced Capps are fine and dandy
But, do not offer the sugar hit Frappuccinos offer.

Regardless, I will still turn to Timmie's
For my morning cup of Joe
Unless the line-up is long again
Then to a nearby McD's I shall go.

First Signing

I was feeling trepidation
While setting up my table
"Will anyone stop by?", I worried.
I was an unknown to this world.

I was surrounded by fellow writers
Ones who had honed their craft
Some accompanied by personal assistants or models
Yet, I was all alone in this environment.

People filed in
As they visited the other booths
I sat at my station and hoped
Someone might be interested in my wares.

Suddenly, a ray of redheaded light
Stopped by to say hello
A face I had not seen in years
A reunion long-awaited.

I ended up selling eight copies that day
Not bad for a first-timer
But, the meeting of my long-lost sister
Made the day fulfillingly complete.

Still Struggling

My road to recovery
Has not been an easy one
I still face mountains of challenges
On a daily basis.

The temptations are constantly in my face
Adverts for the next big jackpot announce
Enticing the sheep to buy-in
For a shot at false security.

I cannot surcumb to these voices
No matter how loud they may be
Because once I place my money down
All abstinance earned will be lost.

It is a constant struggle
Trying to be vigilant
But, everyday stresses and pressures
Make me wonder, "What if?"

So, I do my best to turn a blind eye
To all of the media hype
And, bury myself with new releases
In hopes I can quiet the voices another day.

Southern Seductress

Her voice is as soothing
As a warm summer breeze
Sitting here beside her
Makes me weak to my knees.

I have paid her a visit
After being apart for many months
Getting reacquainted once again
With the woman that I love.

I am introduced to our two fur babies
A Yorkie and a Pom
Both have me wrapped around their paws
Just like their adoring, adoptive Mom.

We prepare the necessary paperwork
To finally start the process going
For me to leave the only home I've known
And, start a new life down in the sun.

It will be months before it is final
But, in the end it will be worth it
Trading the Maple Leaf for Stars and Stripes
So, I can be with my future wife; "Who'da thunk it?"

Summer of Craziness

A huge sporting festival
Unlike anything this city has ever seen
Is about to commence
Throwing commuters in a tizzy.

Highway lanes have been earmarked
For the swarm of transport vehicles
Carrying athletes, media, and spectators
To the various venues.

A new rail link has been built
To sweep visitors to the city downtown
All for the low price of $27.50 for one-way
Gouging at its finest.

For someone in my normal profession
A courier who uses transit to make his deliveries
Navigating will be an absolute zoo
The vehicles will be packed daily.

I only wished I could be elsewhere
During these future five weeks
Preferably a certain destination in Florida
No need to explain why.

The Man With Five Hats

One thing I have found out about myself
Is that I cannot say no
Always taking on new responsibilities
Whenever called upon.

This has led to what my schedule has been
For a recent fortnight
Working long hours every weekday
Complete with travelling to opposite ends of the city.

Five jobs I am working during this period
Courier, Accounting Clerk, and Cleaning Supervisor
Add a temp job as a receptionist
And a volunteer gig preparing income taxes

These are draining jobs
Physically, mentally, and emotionally
Yet, I continue to march to the varying beats
In a way to occupy my time.

I do it in a bid to not resort to my old vice
Thinking, if I'm busy I won't return
Alas, my concern now is due to all the stress
I might break down from exhaustion.

Me Time

With my busy schedule
I find it difficult to take a step back
And, enjoy a few moments
For myself.

Work has me constantly on the go
My 12-step commitments take up more of my time
And, whatever is left
My loving fiancee occupies.

It seems like the only occasion
Where I get the chance to sit down and write
Is when I decide to "play hooky"
From at least one of these life consumers.

I don't like having to shirk responsibilites
So, I could take some time for myself
But, if I want to maintain some grasp on my sanity
This is an unfortunate necessity.

So, I'm camping out in a coffee shop
Typing away on my laptop
And, seeing where my poetic muse
Takes me with my thoughts.

Growing Up Fatherless

Today is a day to celebrate
The paternal influences in our lives
To cherish the male role models
We had growing up.

Some will post messages on social media
With photos and memories of their fathers
Alas, for someone like myself
I cannot share in their sentiments.

For I have spent the past 44 years of my life
Never knowing who my father is
A result from a teenage pregnancy
With possible horrific circumstances.

It pains me to have gone through my life
Not being able to find out his identity
But, if what I fear was the cause of my conception
I can understand why it's been a guarded secret.

So, to wherever and whomever he is
I wish my biological sperm donor a 'Happy Father's Day'
And, may he never forget
The product he left behind unknown.

Ode to The Beautiful Game - 2015

There has been a lot of criticism
As to how this tournament is being played
Forgoing the traditional grass
For an artificial surface.

Be it as it may, 24 nations have assembled
Upon this vast country of ours
To partake in the traditional game of soccer
Or, football as it's better known across the pond.

The tournament began in Edmonton
On a sunny June day
Other cities joined in
To watch the women of the world play.

Thousands will attend the matches
And millions more will watch at home
Showcasing the beauty of the game
And, a nation proud to host.

The tournament will end a month later
In the shadow of the British Columbia Coastal Mountains
And a new champion will be crowned
Hoisting a stylish trophy world-renowned.

Tight Deadline

The clock is ticking
Time is running out
And, the project I'm working on
Is nowhere near finished.

I have set this personal deadline
So, my work could be released to the masses
And, an opportunity
To capitalize on the event at hand.

Yet, my muse seems to be fleeting
He does not want to co-operate
I have the want to write
But, the need is not there.

I will myself
To force the words onto the page
It might seem like utter nonsense
However, it is the best I can do.

Why did I put myself under such pressure?
I always do this to myself
I only hope my intended audience
Enjoy the finished product.

It's A Woman's Romance World

One thing I observed
Among all of the romance author events I see listed
Is that all of the people appearing
Are of the female gender.

I will admit that I'm new
To writing the genre
But, given the numbers
I'm a small fish in an ocean of sharks.

I have heard reports
Males do write romance
However, they do so under cloak and daggar
Wanting to remain faceless names.

I, on the other hand
Decide to go against the grain
Throwing caution to the wind
In hopes I can become known

Alas, when you write two other genres
Things can get complicated
And, makes me wonder
If I should stick to them instead.

Friend-in-Laws

It is no secret
That I'm getting married soon
But, our friends
Are driving us both up the wall.

They constantly badger us with queries
"When are you having the ceremony?"
And, we keep telling them the same answer
"We'll do it when his visa is granted."

I can understand their excitement
As the date draws nearer
However, who is this occassion for?
Us, or them?

Our friends pronounce
They are part of the wedding party
I just don't recall
My bride-to-be and I discussing it.

For now, I must be patient
Willing to accept my future friends for who they are
I only wish with all of the hoopla
We decide to keep the proceedings small.

Rainy Weekend

They say "April showers bring May flowers"
An a propos adage for spring
Alas, when it is the first full weekend of summer
It puts a damper on one's plans.

Patrons on the patios
Are forced indoors
Enjoying their potent potables
Along a crowded bar.

One could enjoy a stroll by the beach
But, only if they have an umbrella in hand
And, hope that flashes of thunder
Do not emerge from the skies overhead.

I, on the other hand,
Have taken sanctuary in my apartment.
Only venturing out
For a couple quick errands.

It does make me feel sad
That this summer weekend has become a wash-out
There is one solace I can take from this,
It is a perfect opportunity to write.

National Celebration

Today is a day
For people across this great land
To celebrate our nation's birthday
And, show how much this place means to us.

Most revellers will enjoy a barbeque
With some frosty beverages
Or, take in the fireworks
Later on in the evening.

However, some people will see this
As a way to relax
Enjoying a day off
From their normal daily grind.

I, myself,
Am enjoying my slice of Canadiana this morn
Coffee and donuts
From a commercial iconic chain.

So, to those who call
The Great White North home
Happy Canada Day to one and all
Just don't drink and drive.

Summer Kickoff

One thing I enjoy
Whenever the calendar nears July
Is the start of a new season
For gridiron fans like me.

Nine teams begin their quest
For Earl Grey's Cup
Eighteen games they must survive
If they want a shot at it.

They fight through all types of weather
Through the months ahead
Because that's how the sport is played
In the most adverse of conditions.

The season ends during the bitter cold
Of a November Sunday eve
But, that is months from now
The coin-toss is afoot.

As always I shall cheer
For my beloved black and gold
And hope for a better result this year
Than the previous two tries.

Working in Discomfort

For weeks now
I have been trying to sit and relax
But, my back is not
Allowing me to do so.

I look like I'm fidgeting
In my seat
Whenever I'm at work or at home
And, I find it quite annoying.

I believe it stems from an incident
When I was working on the road
Hurrying to make a subway train
And, the doors crunched my body.

I know I should go see a specialist
To get it checked out
Alas, that costs money
That I don't have right now.

So, I suffer in discomfort
Trying to stretch my muscles
While popping the odd ibuprofen
In hopes for some relief.

Cloudy Skies

As I sit here enjoying
A day off from work
I look out from my living room window
And, see a dismal summer day.

It had been raining on and off
Ever since the weekend
While I don't mind the precipitation
Enough is enough.

I would love more than anything
To sit out on a patio
Enjoying a summer drink
While my muse inspires me.

Alas, the skies are threatening
With more moisture on the ground
Not the most enticing weather
To be sitting outside.

The temperature is warm though
Perfect for this time of year
But, for a day like today
It's probably better to stay inside.

Reunion Snub

A few weeks ago
My high school class marked 25 years
Since its graduation
However, I was absent from the festivities.

I have no idea
Why I was excluded
I have lived in the same area
As I did back then.

Granted, I had moved
To a new apartment 7 years ago
Yet, I expected someone to reach out
It never happened.

And yes, I was bitter
Over the apparent snub
I thought I was a popular student
This was not the case.

But, I should have taken more initiative
To keep in better contact with the alumni
Instead of being a trivia answer
To the question, "Whatever happened to him?"

The Twelve Steps

I admit it
I am someone who suffers from addiction
The road I've travelled to disarray
Is one that is long and troubled.

Immaturity and procrastination
Are two of my biggest character defects
I never wanted to grow up
Always seeking the easy way out.

However, I am walking a new path
On my road to recovery
And, the course I'm taking
Is done one day at a time.

I seek strength in my brothers and sisters
Of my designated fellowship
Together we gain knowledge
Of what brought us here.

I have had slips along the way
But, I have gotten back on the wagon
Knowing I can never
Go back to where I have been before.

Life As An Indie

I got into this craft
Because I love to write
Sharing my works
For those interested to read them.

I admit I am envious
Of those with the publishing deals
Having a huge promotional machine
Backing their sales.

Alas, I am still an unknown
Toiling away when I can
Writing a multitude of genres
Trying to appeal to everyone's tastes.

I know I can never compete
With the big boys and girls
Yet, I still type away
Creating worlds on my laptop.

If I can generate a fan base
And, net some sales along the way
All the better in the long run.
But, for now, I enjoy being an indie author.

Sereni-tea

As a writer, I am always looking for fuel
Some liquid refreshment
To power my way
Through a scene or a verse.

While nowadays this is generated
By the caffeinated bean
Once in a while I enjoy
The relaxing steep of the dried leaf.

My pantry is filled
With many varieties of tea
Flavours abound the shelves
To tempt my palate.

Logic would dictate
That I should chill my product
However, one can not discount
A hot 'cuppa' on a day like today.

I have settled on a festive rooibos
And, sip while I finish this stanza
A calm fills me inside
My muse is finally at peace.

Summer Construction

There is a saying
We have here in Canada
"We are a country of two seasons:
Winter and construction."

No truer an example of the latter
Can be seen on the sidestreets
Near my apartment
As crews work around the day.

We have a crumbling infrastructure
Which makes this all necessary
However, for motorists alike
It is only a pain in the rear.

Equipment litters the roads
As they dig up the ground
Replacing decaying watermains
Before water floods the area.

It is a tell-tale sign
The city has been lax in their repairs
But, the question I ask is
"What took them so long?"

Delinquents

With the calendar rolling into July
It means only one thing
School is out for summer
And, children have too much time on their hands.

Try as parents must
To find ways for their kids
To occupy their time
All of their efforts fail.

They do not want them
Stuck indoors all day watching television
Or, playing on the computer
Exercise and fresh air is a necessity.

However, they want them to stay close
To their home nowadays
For fear predators are lurking
Around every corner.

So, they resort to outright hooliganism
As a way to entertain themselves
Pulling every fire alarm in the building
Making those who work from home suffer.

Hallowed Lawns

There are different playing fields
In the world of sports
But, none more famous
Than an array of grass courts in England.

Late June and early July
Bring the best in the world
At the game of tennis
To the Lawn and Croquet Club in suburban London.

Legendary players have dominated
The lawns at this hallowed place
Names like Federer and Williams
As well as, Graf and Borg.

They held the Olympic tournament here
A mere three years ago
A second opportunity for these purveyors
To make their mark here.

And, when all is said and done
The famous trophies are presented
And, the winners will forever
Be etched into tennis history.

Under Further Review

One thing authors utilize
To see whether or not
People like their work
Is to receive a review from a reader.

I have seen my friends garner
Numerous of these
However, a heartless corporation
Is threatening to take them away.

They claim these words of praise
Are not true in their eyes
Alleging there is favouritism
Because the reviewer "knows" the author.

Many feel this is a bid of censorship
A way to bury the independents
And, give priority to
The big publishing house writers.

I confess I have received
Very little words of praise
But, if they take them away
No one will know who I am.

Blowout in the 'Peg

I came home from work
On an early July Thursday
And, turned on the television
To watch my beloved Black and Gold.

They were playing on the road
In the Manitoba capital
Hoping they would bounce back
From a last-second loss in Cowtown last week.

What has unfolded
Is a complete decimation of their opponent
Who had shocked the league
By defeating their heated rival in their opening game.

Pick-Sixes and punt returns
Taken back to the house
Have made my team
Light up the scoreboard.

I begin to feel a slight remorse
For the Blue and Gold-clad opposition
But, secretly wish for a similar result
When they play in The Hammer next month.

The Final Straw

I have been a loyal employee
Of my primary place of employment
For almost two years
But, I'm ready to say, "enough is enough".

I have always done
Everything they have asked of me
However, lately my employers
Have been taking advantage of my good nature.

Today was probably the straw
That broke this camel's back
And, I am ready to
Pack things in with them.

I don't mind doing
Long runs to the middle of nowhere
Unfortunately, the one they sent me on today
Was too much for anyone to do by foot.

I will use the weekend
To explain it is time for me to move on
Beginning to prepare for
The big steps to come.

Ode To My Future Home

Tomorrow marks the day
Where those south of the 49th
Celebrate their nation's birthday
With the same grandeur we celebrate ours.

Cookouts and fireworks
Will be the course of their day
As well as, waving the Stars and Stripes
To show their patriotic nature.

Americans tend to go
More "all out" on Independence Day
I can't say I blame them
They have been around longer than us.

The one thing I do have to
Prepare for in the next few months
Is to adopt the style and culture
Of my future homeland.

It will be tough
Trading a beaver for an eagle
But, one thing I won't mind
Is having all the Wheaties I can handle.

Relaxing by the Pool

A friend of mine posted a photo
Of herself lounging by a swimming pool
And, it made me envious
Of her being in such a setting.

I used to love hanging out
In the chlorinated water
A throwback to my days
As a competitive swimmer.

It has been 21 years
Since I retired my Speedos
But, I still yearn to be
Lounging on the deck nearby.

On a day like today
It would be an utmost serene scene
Sitting in a deck chair
Typing out another stanza.

However, upon further reflection
It might not be a good idea
My laptop would get wet
Thus, losing all of my hard work.

Why So 'Jelly'?

I have to confess
That I'm jealous of my friends
Being able to go away for summer holidays
While I'm stuck toiling away at work.

I should not be complaining
As I had a two-week vacation in April
To see my beloved in Florida
And, get reacquainted once again.

I admit the timing could have been better
But, we had not seen each other in months
A visit long overdue
Because we missed being together.

However, the trip was necessary
To get some valuable paperwork filed
Paving the way to a new chapter
In my life to be written.

I only wish she could come see me
In the weeks ahead
Alas, she's going to a reunion in Iowa
While I toil away at the salt mines.

The Witching Hour

The time has come
For most people to be in bed
Dreaming various worlds
As they drift off to sleep.

Alas, this is the hour
When a writer's creativity
Decides to come out to play
Filling their head with an army of plot bunnies.

The creator of these ideas
Needs to get them down on paper
As soon as possible
Otherwise, they would be lost forever.

Countless amounts of caffeine
Will be consumed by the scribe
In a bid to strike
While the iron is hot.

There have been tales
Of an author suffering sleepless nights
All for the love of capitalizing on
The next big plot twist.

New Toy For The Boy

I don't understand why
Humans of the male gender
Are fascinated with the need
To obtain new technology.

This was the instance yesterday
When my current living companion
Wanted to trade-in his old mobile phone
For a new sleeker model.

He complained about how
He could never hear the ringtone on his former device
Or, the fact he could never get a sense
Of it nestling within his pocket.

The salesperson cut him an awesome deal
On a new handset
Just like a similar model
One of his colleagues at his work possesses.

Now, he is overjoyed to have in his clutches
A new toy to play with
The only drawback to such a find
Is that I have to teach him how to use it.

Writing Sprint

When a budding writer
Is faced with a challenge of composing
X-amount of words within Y-amount of time
They do whatever it takes to obtain them.

A helpful tool in creating
Copious numbers of verbage
Is to engage in an act
Of mindless typing of possible incoherence.

They set out to do this
In short little bursts of creativity
Whether it be 10 or 15 minutes
In a bid to log as many words as they can.

During the frenzied period of November
My bretheren call these "Word Wars"
However, the only opponent I find
Is oneself versus the clock.

So, we write like the wind
In hopes any of it makes sense
Production is the goal at this juncture
The editing will come much later.

An Endless Quest

Recently, an actress my special girl and I
Are interested in
Released her memoirs for fans
Detailing her career while growing up.

The book was touted
With much fanfare from our fandom
As the days drew closer
To the book's eventual release.

I had originally ordered a copy
For my electronic reading device
Alas, a couple weeks before
The option was made unavailable to consumers.

I went on a mad search
At the local major bookstore chain
Hoping to secure a copy for myself
But, was turned away empty both times I tried.

In the end I turned online
To score copies for my love and myself
With a special difference
My darling's copy will be signed by the author.

Sunday Tradition

There are many traditions
That fall upon the so-called Day of Rest
Whether they be spiritual or sports-oriented
We hold them true to our hearts.

In the Autumn, the ritual
Revolves around action on a field
A war of attrition
Is enjoyed by those on this side of the pond.

Other times of the year
It involves an act of reaching out
To one's Higher Power
Praying to them for forgiveness for the week's sins.

However, my Sunday schedule
Does not consist of football, or church
But, camping out in my bedroom
And, firing up Skype on my laptop.

For it is this day
I video chat with my darling love
And, that hour we are together
Makes up for the many miles we are apart.

A Life of Triads

They always say
Things come along in threes
I did not realize this applies
To two different facets of my life.

When it comes to employment
I hold three positions within my company
All specific tasks
Requiring a different skill set for each.

The other pertains to my writing
As I scribe under a trio of monikers
It can be a challenge to know
Which project I'm working on for which.

However, not everything in my life
Has to come in triplicate
Wherever I've lived previously has been a duo
Myself and another person, whether it be family or
roommate.

But, there is one other example
Where the Rule of Three is not followed
The fiancee I'm with is my second
And, I intend her to be my first wife for eternity.

The Boys of Summer

As I sit here alone at home
While my roommate is out with his friend
I am typing away on my laptop
A baseball game on our television.

I think back to the days of my youth
Spending a leisurely weekend day
Down by the waterfront
Watching the Jays at the Exhibition.

It is hard to believe it has been
Sixteen years since they have moved
From the so-called 'Mistake By The Lake"
To the retractable roof they play under now.

Many highlight seasons have been played
Under the cavernous dome
But, I still yearn for the days
Sitting under the covered grandstand at the Ex.

The Grounds have changed dramatically
In the years that have passed
But, I still love my Jays
Even if I do not go as often as I used to.

Tall, Frosty One

On a hot day like today
There is nothing I would enjoy
More than a cold beer
It would refresh me dramatically.

The only problem is
With the vast array of brands to choose from
I cannot decide which company's pint
I should settle upon.

Do I go for an ale or a lager?
Perhaps, a light Pilsner?
The selection is endless
Over at the retailer a block away.

I admit I have my favourites
When it comes to alcoholic suds
But, I also like to be adventurous
Willing to try something new.

I check my wallet
Alas, I'm strapped for cash
Instead, I head to the refrigerator
And, pour myself a cold glass of water.

The Countdown Is On

When I started on this journey
I thought it was going to be forever
Funny how circumstances can
Change things in an instant.

I have gone above and beyond
The call of duty for them
However, all they have done
Is take advantage of me.

I want to thank them for
Everything they have provided
But, in the same breath
They have taken away my time and energy.

After all of the stress they've given
All of the free time they have taken away
The time has finally come
To say goodbye to them.

I am not asking for much
Just a 'thank you for your service'
Regardless of what transpires
In a matter of days, I will be gone.

The Animal Within

As the night draws in
And, the moon rises in the sky
The wolf within me
Seeks to go out on the prowl.

My prey sits next to me
Snuggled upon the couch
She gives me an adoring look
But, with a hint of lustful hunger.

We stare into each other's eyes
Giving a silent nod
We make our way to the bedroom
For a night of carnal delight.

Our passion is heated
As we make love between the sheets
Devouring each other senseless
We become one this eve.

After our deed has been done
Holding our loves in our arms
We know we were meant to be
Together for all eternity.

She Looks Good To Me

I have to admit something
There are very few things
That bring much joy
Into my humble life.

However, there is a ray
Of sun-kissed Florida sunshine
That turns my gloomy days
Into the brightest of them all.

Her voice is like that of
Southern angels descending from above
And, when I hear her dulcet tones
It makes my heart sing along with her.

I look forward to our Skype chats
When I can see her beautiful face.
I can see her hazel eyes sparkle
Whenever she sees my face.

She is my true vision of beauty
A woman near and dear to me
Something I am reminded of
Everytime I turn on my laptop.

Finding The Will (To Write)

I find myself
Crashed out on my bed
My back is once again
Causing me grief.

After a long day of working
I feel the need to rest
However, my current project
Is crying for attention.

I debate about taking a nap
A few minutes will not hurt
But, I know if I snooze
The creative opportunity will be lost.

My muse feigns cohesiveness
As I lazily type on my keypad
Trying to find some way
For my words to make sense.

Admittedly, the weather does not help
As rain has fallen all afternoon
And, my spirit is as dreary
As the skies overhead.

In The Spotlight

One thing an artist craves for
Is to be featured on center stage
With all the eyes of the audience
Cast upon them.

It does not matter if you're a dancer
An actress, or a writer
They all desire to be
At the forefront of attention.

This is the time where they
Must seize the moment of opportunity
For the light will only
Be shining on them for a few minutes.

Will they rise to the occasion?
Or, wilt under the pressure?
The only way to know
Is to observe how they handle themselves.

Their time is now
There is no turning back
Because as soon as the turn is over
Their time has passed them by.

The Thunder Returns

Dark skies are cast
Upon the heavens overhead
And, a distant rumble
Can be heard from miles away.

Rain drops are falling
Dampening the ground below
Pedestrians take cover
As not to be soaked to their core.

Flashes of lightning
Fill the skies above
Putting on a majestic light show
Only Mother Nature can perform.

The winds have begun to howl
The ferocity of the storm is nearing its apex
Only a matter of time
Until all serenity outdoors is lost.

However, I am the type
Who enjoys this type of weather
Seeking an inspirational power
Of the magnitude of the tempest.

Breaking The Fourth Wall

There is an unspoken rule
In the world of the arts
One should never acknowledge
The existence of the audience.

They are there to witness
The proceedings of the production
But, the performers should not
Talk to them directly.

I find it odd where some people
Do so in a tongue-in-cheek fashion
Almost as if they want them in
On whatever joke is being played.

Does this rule apply to the world
Of the poetic arts and prose?
Because the work should be to
Engage the reading public.

Regardless of what one thinks
I have to nod to my readers here
Thank you for sticking through this far
This collection is halfway complete.

Swan Song

The word is out
Everyone at work knows
That I am in my final days
As a colleague.

The sentiments are trickling in
Most of them say I will be missed
Where I was a valuable asset to the company
My contribution will be lost.

I must confess
It will be a sad day when
The business closes on
The last Friday of the month.

I vowed to stay in touch
It is the least I could do
The company gave me so much
During the past two years.

I am still dreading what they might
Do to me in the next few weeks
But, the absent camaraderie afterwards
Will leave a hole in my soul.

Alternative Fuel

Many a time I have
Praised my devotion to the bean
However, fluids are not the only thing
That power a writer's words.

In the fits of frenzied writing
Solid sustinance is necessary
To keep the scribe's mind
Energized and creative.

While I admit it is not
Part of a healthy diet
A good portion of snacks does help
Whether they be sweet, or salty.

I make no denial
Of my love for chocolate and peanut butter
A remarkable combination
That satisfies both my cravings.

Alas, I am fresh out
Of such a supply
Thankfully, my roommate is generous
And, to nosh on, has brought me some pie.

Vinyl Collectibles

There are many things
A collector can covet
However, none are more extensive
Than the one my roommate possesses.

He has amassed a treasure trove
Of vinyl figurines detailing pop culture
But, are more geared towards
His taste in cable television heroines.

One set is based on a single character
From a popular medieval-set series
Done up in various costumes
She had adorned over the seasons.

The other set features an actress
From a show where she plays a multitude of characters
Some of which display
Various amounts of damage a role has suffered.

One would think I would roll my eyes
Over such an array of collectibles
But, I confess I own one of my own
From a popular movie last year.

Feeling The Heat

With the summer days
Come heat and humidity
Both uncomfortable elements
Of the season.

It is days like these
Where we crave to be indoors
Finding needed relief
Thanks to the benefit of air conditioning.

Alas, I do not currently live
In an apartment with such a luxury
Relying completely upon
A small fan beside my bed.

I know things will change
Once I move in with my future wife
Where it will be hot all year around
And cool rooms will be a necessity.

Until then, I will have to suffer
And, consume copious amounts of water
As well as, take the odd cold shower
In a bid to fight off heat stroke.

Craving Camaraderie

Because of my long hours at work
I have not been able to
Hang out with my friends
And, socialize while we write.

It has been a Friday tradition
During three months of the year
Where we gather at a midtown coffee shop
To type and cause merriment.

It is something I have not
Been able to do for a few weeks
Runs to the middle of nowhere
Have prevented me from reuniting with them.

I will say a solemn prayer tonight
In hopes there is not a repeat of seven days before
Where I was sent to the northeast part of the region
My return home was not until late.

I want to sit and scribe
Trying to concentrate through the noise
An escape from work for once
So, I can let my muse thrive again.

Apologies To My Compatriots

I do not know what is wrong with me
I had a golden opportunity to
Reunite with my comrades
Only to stand them up in the end.

All of the stars had aligned
For me to join up with them
I had gotten out of work early
With no long-distance runs logged.

I was set to change out of my work clothes
Grab my notepad and pens
And, boot it to the coffee shop
However, something made me change my mind.

Was it the fact I was too tired from work?
Am I scared to tell them I'll be unemployed soon?
Yes, it is probably the latter
I was always one who is concerned with my image.

Regardless of the circumstances
I am writing in my room
Perhaps, I wanted some serenity
Only home could provide.

Blowing Off

There has been many a time
When I had scheduled something
To do with my roommate
Only to have my plans thrown in disarray.

It was always something I wanted to do together
However, he would make his own plans
Whether it was a trip across the border
Or, a party with his friends.

I would be disappointed
Having to go alone
But, in the end I ended up enjoying
The event I wound up attending.

Now, the shoe is on the other foot
He wants us to do something together
Alas, it is not an event
I have any interest in.

Instead, I will be heading
Out of town for the evening
For once, I'm blowing him off
Let's see how he feels about it.

Sweaty Bawls

It is summertime in the city
And, the humidity is unbearable
Unless you have air conditioning
One must be subject to the heat.

There is no worse place to be
During the hot temperatures
Than, a crowded transit vehicle
Where the A/C has not kicked in.

I try to cool down with a beverage
While holding onto a handrail
But, it is not easy to drink and balance
On a jerking subway train.

I press up against the glass
In a bid to stabilize myself
The car is so warm
Sweat from my arm stains the window.

I pray for my stop to come soon
Or, for some travellers to get off
Alas, it would not be the case
And, my ride is spent in discomfort.

Everyday Struggle

It is not easy to be
Someone battling an addiction
When everywhere you go
Advertisements attempt to entice.

They tout all of the ways
You could feed your vice
All with one simple investment
Into their sinful products.

They claim the payoff would be huge
If only you bought into it
But, I know it would only cause
More problems than they would solve.

I remind myself I have to
Remain vigilant to my recovery
Because one small slip
Will take me back down that dark road.

I had been there before
And, it was not a happy place
I need to reach out to my Higher Power
Praying for the vice to find some different space.

Competitive Renaming

I understand with any
International sporting event
There will be renaming of some venues
To wash away any corporate affiliation.

Personally, I find it to be a waste
To scrub the facilities of their known monikers
Only to appease the big wigs
Who are the official licenced sponsors.

Everyone will still call the sites
By their traditional names
Not some convoluted venue title
That has only a temporary placement.

The "Pan Am Dome" will
Always be known to us
As "Rogers Centre" or "SkyDome"
So, officials need to cut the crap.

And, I intend to enjoy my soccer
Tomorrow night in Hamilton
Who knows? I might enjoy a double-double
Just to piss the organizers off.

A Beautiful Night in The Hammer

There are very few places
I can call a second home
A city where I feel calm
Away from my apartment in Toronto.

I have travelled fifty miles
Due southwest, along the lakeshore
And, I can breathe a relaxed sigh
Amid the steel mill smokestacks

As the train pulls into West Harbour
I know I have arrived
As I look over the water
Seeing the Skyway in the distance.

This town was the founding place
Of a Canadian cultural icon
The double-doubles taste more special
From the first store on Ottawa Street North.

While the sun sets over the west bleachers
Of the new football stadium
I am at peace with where I am
Where Steeltown is my adopted home.

Another Humid Sunday

The mercury in the thermometer
Tells me it is a scorcher today
The only comfort I have
Is a fan oscillating in my living room.

The temperature states
We are in the eighties
But, I can imagine it feels much warmer
When you factor in the humidity.

A fellow writer had a good idea
To read by the side of a pool
Alas, the only chlorinated water I can access
Requires an admission fee to get in.

I debate about stripping down
And, taking a cool shower
However, that would only provide me
Some temporary relief.

So, I sit with the fan blowing on me
My laptop wide open, as I type
My television on the Pan Ams coverage
I suppose things could be worse.

Ambitious Task

When I set out on this literary quest
To scribe 90 poems in 30 days
It did not occur to me
The need for inspiration had to be constant.

I have done the best I can
Given the circumstances
But, on a day where I have time to write
My muse seems to have disappeared.

I could always tap into
Some of my previous works
However, that would be going against
My literary morals.

I flip the channels on my television
And, read the newspaper
Trying to come up with new ideas
Alas, the well is running dry.

So, I turn to a poetic rant
About how the words can be fleeting
Hoping they would come back
Before my calendar runs out.

Quadrennial Political Circus

If there is one thing I'm dreading
When I move to my new home
Is the media circus that revolves
Around their political offices.

I should be no stranger
To the mudslinging that goes on
It has started to pop-up on the airwaves
Here in my current hometown.

However, where I am headed
They tend to be more cutthroat
Spewing attack ads about
Their heated rivals.

The big one always seems to happen
The same year the Summer Games take place
But, there are ones that occur on a different cycle
And, that worries the heck out of me.

I was never one
To have things shoved down my throat
Alas, where I will be going
I should prepare for a steady diet of political B.S.

Disputing Views

In my therapy the other day
I informed my group I was leaving my job
So, I could concentrate upon
My upcoming emigration.

I told them I would not be leaving
For another couple of months, I figured
But, when the time arrives
The change will happen fast.

This alarmed one of my brothers
Who was worried about my recovery
Trying to burden me with employment legalese
About approaching it a different way.

He told me I should have taken
A leave of absence from work
Sort my crap out with my case first
And, not walk away completely.

The problem is, he doesn't know
I'm doing this more for me
One cannot prepare to leave
When their mind is occupied with stress.

A Crafty Relationship

My fiancee and I
Are two artistic people
But, we are our own masters
At our different crafts.

I construct worlds with my words
Typing out images in my mind's eye
In hopes my readership
Would be entertained with my descriptions.

She, on the other hand,
Makes her own visual art
Stitching and snipping
Her work is a feast for the eyes.

Whether it is cross-stitching
Or, making bookmarks and magnets
My love has a flair for her work
Her hands create tirelessly.

The two of us make a valuable team
A pair of artists who strive
To bring our work to a small mass
And, hope we will be appreciated for it.

Body Breakdown

I know I am getting old
It is inevitable for all of us
I only thought it would not happen to me
For a few years yet.

My back is in need of constant stretching
Or, a soothing massage
Alas, the only person I want touching me
Is in another country at the present.

I also feel pain in my joints
My knee, wrists, and elbow
If I am afflicted with arthritis
Then, rain might be on its way.

I ought to know that I cannot keep
Running on limited sleep
As my body cannot handle
Going without proper rest.

The problem is I think of myself
As someone of middle-age
But, one thing I am not ready to do yet
Is slow my lifestyle down.

Nap Time

My eyes are growing heavy
And, my mind is not as sharp
A tell-tale sign of lack of sleep
Is starting to catch up to me.

I fight the need to lie down
Wanting to scribe more words
However, they are slow in coming
My writing is becoming faulted.

I thought I learned my lesson
After my train trip last September
Alas, with me, old habits die hard
And, I continue to struggle to write.

It does not help that I am distracted
By the television and social media
All of what they say is a blur
As I drift in and out of consciousness.

I save my work, and turn off the power
Heading towards my room
A nap will refresh me, I figure
In hopes my muse will return.

The Next Step

There was much elation yesterday
When my fiancee checked her mail
A long awaited letter
Telling us the next actions to take.

She had done her part
To forward the necessary data
So, I would have everything
On my end for the interview.

The onus is on me now
To jump through the next set of hoops
I had dragged my heels before
I do not want to disappoint her.

I was up until late last night
Completing a portion of the required elements
The rest will come soon
Over the next few weeks.

It is an arduous task
But, worth it in the end
The moment is nigh
When I can call her my wife.

Together We Are One

She and I are a cohesive unit
Always there for each other
She will have my back
And, I will have hers.

We cheer each other up
When the other is feeling blue
A love like no other we share
Our emotions we share are true.

We might be a distance apart
However, when we are together, it is magic
An experience unlike any other
Our hearts are in sync.

We long for the day
When that space is forever minimized
A moment when we can walk hand-in-hand
Down the sidewalk of her neighbourhood.

We know we are meant to be
Two hearts beating as one
We long for the day
When we will never be alone again.

Incoherent Muse

Sometimes when I write
I have a problem
Trying to transfer the words I think
Onto the page I'm writing.

I find I have the same dilemma
Whenever I attempt to speak
The words I say
Are not always the ones in my head.

It can easily occur
Whenever I am distracted by other things
My attention is being diverted
To someone else attempting to get to me.

I know some writers
Cannot work with background noise
Alas, I come from a breed where others
Are constantly vying for attention while I scribe.

It is a Catch-22
In my bid for creativity
Sometimes I can come up with great ideas
And, others my mind draws blank.

Evil Allure

The commercials are endless
Advertising the big prizes
Enticing people to buy-in
For a chance at vast riches.

As someone who has such a weakness
I need to be extra vigilant
To not give into the succubus' song
A risk to throw my recovery away.

It knows when my guard is down
It has happened before
I still live down the events of Montreal
Within my mind and soul.

This is why I have to be strong
Not giving into my old vice
Because I know the damage it has done
And, believe me, it is not nice.

I decide to change the channel
Alas, the ad comes on again
I shut off the television
Returning my attention to my new craft.

Giving Back

I have always been a believer
In giving back to the community
Doing something that helps out
Those who are in need.

Volunteering your time
To people who require a hand
Is a rewarding experience
And, subconsciously boosts your outlook.

I do admit there are some organizations
Who will exploit your good nature
Doing so to skirt around
Paying their employees a fair wage.

I have little respect for those
Companies who use such a ploy
But, for those on the up-and-up
It is all the worthwhile in the end.

It provides valuable credentials
Upon your resume
And, that can open doors
To a paying gig in the field.

Fire in the Water

Watching the swimming competition
At the Pan American Games
Makes me feel nostalgic for
When I used to strap on the swimsuit.

While my disciplines were
Geared more to the Para-Pan Ams
I can still appreciate
The dedication the athletes have.

I only wished my work schedule
Would have permitted me to attend
Some of the events this year
As the pool is only minutes away.

The passion and fire
These competitors have are similar
To the same that burned within me
All those years ago.

So, best of luck to the racers
As they swim like they have not swum before
The podium is within reach
The medals are theirs for the taking.

Inconsiderate Neighbours

Bang! Slam! Bang! Slam!
These are the noises that surround my apartment
And, it is quite distracting to me
While I'm trying to write.

I do not know what possesses
Some people to make
Such a racket with their abodes
Are they trying to make a statement?

Is it the work of unruly children
Attempting to get the attention
Of their parents who are ignoring them?
Or, are they misbehaving?

And, what of the ones
Who slam the doors to their units?
I checked outside
It doesn't appear the wind got a hold of it.

Regardless of the noise
I'll be glad to be out of here soon
Where the only distraction
Will be the yips of my fur babies.

Worst Announcer

I often enjoy watching
Canadian football games on the tele
However, there is one commentator
That makes me cringe whenever I hear him.

He is the network's answer
To Captain Obvious
Stating assorted factoids
We, the audience, already know.

He also possesses a complete
Lack of tact in interviewing
Asking uncomfortable questions
At the most inopportune of times.

I will go through withdrawals from the game
But, this is one broadcaster
I will not miss when
I leave this country.

His smug face
And, know-it-all nature
Make him, in my opinion
The biggest douche in Canadian sports.

Can't Feel My Face

When the howling winds of winter
Blow through the city
It chills people to the bone
And, makes their teeth chatter.

However, it is currently
The Dog Days of Summer
Yet, my face is experiencing
The same type of numbness.

One would be led to believe
I had finished a dental visit
The novacaine had yet to wear off
Freezing my muscles in the process.

But, this not the case
As, I had received a clean bill of health
During my last check-up
A few weeks ago.

No, I can't feel my face
Because I'm grinning ear-to-ear
Thinking about the special lady
Who brings much joy to my life.

So Bad, It's Good

Have you ever watched
A movie on television, or in the theatre
Where it is so awful
It is hilarious in the process?

This is the case
Of a certain niche film franchise
Where the concept is outlandish
Yet, people still tune in to watch.

I think it is akin
To the car-crash mentality
Where you know it will be gruesome
But, you cannot turn away when you pass by.

However, the notion of
Such a thing occuring in real-life
Appears so ludicrous
However, our curiousity is piqued.

I mention this because I saw an ad
For the third film being aired next week
Many will be tuning in to see it.
I won't be one of them.

Unwarranted Anxiety

I do not know why I am
Nervous about what is to come
I have nothing to worry about
Or, do I?

I have handled navigating
This maze of red tape, so far
Yet, it is what is ahead of me
That has me concerned.

I am doing my part
To gather the necessary documentation
I will admit the Police Certificate
Has me a little antsy.

But, I have had no prior convictions
I am pretty much a saint
However, there is one thing about the process
That is raising alarm bells.

It is where they want me to book the interview
A city I am all too familiar with
It is the site of my last relapse
That is what the problem is.

The Final Fortnight

After the day I had today
I was glad there are only two weeks left
However, after settling down
I am re-evaluating my feelings.

I know I said I was leaving
And, it is for the best
I only want to go
Without any bitterness within me.

Yes, being on the road can be stressful
When they are sending you everywhere
But, the dispatchers are doing the best they can
Given the roster they are handed daily.

I have noticed they are cutting down
The boundaries of where they send us
I wonder, though, if it is because
They are losing a valuable asset soon.

Regardless, I will continue to do my job
Finishing off my tenure
I will miss being out in the city
I will not miss the stress, though.

Rainy Night in Bytown

The skies have opened up
In the community known as The Glebe
And the walk down to Lansdowne Park
Requires a raincoat.

It would be easy
To pop open an umbrella
Alas, security would confiscate it
Upon entry into the stadium.

If you sit on the north side
You have the benefit of the roof overhang
While those on the south side
Will get soaked in their seats.

There will always be the banter
About which side sucks
But, they are there for a common reason
To cheer on "Le Rouge et Noir".

At the end, they will head home
Another game in the books
While I sit in another city
Craving for a Beavertail.

Forest City Reunion

I will be returning
To a city I know well
To reunite with some of my fellow writers
Who I first met here in Toronto.

The event will have
A Roaring 20's motif
Complete with a request to cosplay
As flapper girls at the After Party.

Alas, I cannot stay around
As my bus back home leaves
Right after the main signing
I will miss out on the festivities.

However, there is something else
I am weary of regarding the event
Is a possible face-to-face meeting
I am hoping to avoid.

This city is where the woman I dated
Before I met my fiancee lives
We haven't spoken in months
And, I'm praying that streak continues.

Making Excuses

This burst of writing
Was my first in three days
Not something a serious writer
Ought to have been doing.

I am envious of my friends
Who could output thousands of words a day
But, they have the benefit
Of not having a steady form of employment.

Yes, I know some of them
Tend to their children while
Their spouses make a living wage
They are the lucky ones.

I know my time is coming
When I will have more free time on my hands
Where I can be alone with my thoughts
And, be able to put them down on paper.

Alas, for now I must bide my time
And, try to scribe when I can
However, I have deadlines to meet soon
I do not want to go back on my word.

Signature Abomination

As I have been watching
The games of this weekend
A couple of the teams have donned their
Alternate uniforms they unveiled last year.

I remember seeing them months ago
In my opinion, a few of them were alright
Alas, the rest of them, the designer
Ought to have been shot.

My roommate and I both agree
These abominations should not
Have seen the light of day
Instead, having gone back to the drawing board.

I know this was all a marketing ploy
In a bid to boost slagging apparel sales
I wonder whose profit margin they were trying to pad
The league's, or the manufacturer's?

For myself, I prefer the normal jerseys
The teams don on regular gamedays
No tweaks or radical designs necessary
Just clean-cut jerseys and pants.

Closing Ceremony Flap

There has been a huge controversy
Regarding a performer
Headlining the Closing Ceremonies
At the current Pan Am Games.

People have been complaining
That it ought to have been a Canadian act
Closing the show
A short in event planning.

However, I have to shake my head
At those who are doing all the griping
Asking them some valid questions
About why they are whining.

Are they actually going to the event?
If so, leave before he comes on.
If not, then why are they kvetching?
They are not paying to attend the show.

My advice is if they are planning on watching
From the comforts of their own home
Turn the channel before he comes on
You do have that choice.

Summer's First Hot Day

Until today, the temperature
Has been rather comfortable
Warm, but not all that humid
Still managable for most.

However, the mercury has risen
Over 30 degrees Celcius today
Factor in the humidity
And, it feels as hot as a human's normal temperature.

I crave for some air conditioning
While I write in my living room
Alas, my only reliefs are
A bottle of water and a single fan.

One might think I am daft
For trying to type in this heat
But, my project is due soon
I cannot ease up for a moment.

I feel for those who have
To work outside in this
I hope and pray they won't succumb
To a case of heat stroke on the job.

A Slight Miscalculation

Earlier in this collection
I made reference to a certain poem
Being the halfway mark of the tome
Alas, I confess I made a grave error.

The premise was to write
Ninety poems within thirty days
However, that was including
Thirteen poems I had written beforehand.

To make amends to myself
I have decided to extend the project
So, it can be a proper 90 in 30
And, my conscience can rest easier.

In the end, this collection
Will have a grand total of 103 sonnets
A reasonable improvement
On my previous two releases.

Although, I do realize
This poem could be seen as cheap filler
But, like an activist once spoke
"By any means necessary."

The Makeshift Ballyard

Tomorrow, my roommate and I
Will be making a short trip east
To take in the Bronze Medal Game
Of the Pan Am Baseball tournament.

When I first heard of the event
I thought the games would be played
On an existing diamond, like Christie Pits.
Alas, this was not to be the case.

Instead, they are being contested
At a new facility in the Town of Ajax
Where the tickets are being sold
On a General Admission basis.

The thing that concerns me
Is where the park is situated
North of a sinful venue
I know all too well.

I will be fortunate to be shuttled
From the train station to the ballyard
And, I will not end up losing
What little recovery I have maintained.

Broken Bobblehead

There is a little bobblehead doll
I use to say goodbye to my fiancee
Whenever we finish using Skype
However, something happened to it.

A few weeks ago
The adhesive glue on the inside of the doll
Came undone from the head
Now, it bobbles askew.

I need to get a new one
So, we may continue our tradition
The only problem is
I'm not sure if there is a place that still has one.

It is odd to say the character's
Signature catchphrase while
Shaking a broken bobblehead
His head resembles the Leaning Tower of Piza.

It is a matter of actually getting out
To conduct my search
The only question is if I find one of him
Do I get the similar style, or a different one?

Diabetic Dilemma

I have stated numerous times
About one of my worst vices
One that I have been in recovery for
The past couple of years.

However, there is another weakness I have
And, one could argue it's purely emotional
But, like the the one I seek guidance of
It is one that is detrimental to my health.

I speak about my addiction to carbs
Whether sugar, or complex
Breads and desserts I crave
Whenever I feel at an emotional low.

I never considered myself such an eater
Alas, it does make a perfect diagnosis
If I feel sad, I load up on sweets and starches
An escape in so-called 'comfort food'.

I know I need to control those urges
Being mindful of my diet
I'm already suffering from Type-II
I do not want to deteriorate even more.

My Steamy Side

There has been a persona of mine
I've tried to keep quiet
But, recently I decided
To make it become known.

It is for a genre of writing
My family might not approve of
Because it is saucier
Than their usual literary tastes.

However, I find it integral
As part of my triad of writing
Three different names
For three different core genres.

I only make mention of this now
For I had been sidetracked from this
To answer the calling voice
And, my steamy side awakens again.

A short had been penned
Not a very long piece
Thirty-one hundred words
Of an erotic fantasy short story.

Bad Food Choices

One thing I admit I love
Is spicy food
Not so much flavour
As it is for heat.

Tonight for dinner I consumed
A pasta dish with some kick
Seasoned with some green chilis
For a decent bit of spice.

Alas, I am now battling
An acute case of indigestion
Something I thought my body could handle
It cannot anymore.

I hope this won't play havoc
On my digestive system overnight
I'm all out of Pepto
And, I don't feel like changing my shorts yet.

So, I'll reach for some antacid
In hopes it will calm my upset stomach
I only hope this will not lead
To an ulcer later on in life.

Living in Her Shadow

When I created my
Steamy writing persona
I did it to follow in the footsteps
Of one of my good friends in the genre.

She has received success
In leaps and bounds
Probably because she has produced
Countless books in the gerne.

However, she still gets frustrated
Whenever someone returns her books
I admit I would be pissed, too
If they wanted a refund for 99 cents.

That being said
She has a devout fan base
Something that makes me jealous
Of her popularity.

Maybe my pen name
Was too close to hers
That's why they chose to read the original
Instead of some wannabe, like me.

Tuesday Night Blahse

As I sit here
Trying to find the words to write
I find myself feeling bored
Struggling to entertain myself.

The night's sports selection
Is limited at best
Baseball doesn't seem to compel me
After the thriller I saw a couple days before.

My fiancee is keeping to herself
Nervous of her annual pilgrimage
To visit her dog rescue resort friends
Worried about having to fly again.

And, my roommate is still not home
He's either working late or out
Although, he can be a pain
I miss the companionship.

Instead, I sit here
Fighting the urge to call it a night early
By whining about it on paper
At least, that is something.

Another Late Night

As I sit here, watching the Jays on the tube
I notice that it is well after 10 at night
And, my roommate has yet
To come home from work.

I know he has been working
Very long hours as of late
But, I also know he's the type
Who likes to socialize with his colleagues.

The only problem is
I know of his vices
The type which lead to
Unhealthy behaviour on his part.

I pray this is not the case
Tonight, or any night
The vice almost led to his demise
Five years ago.

It's a place I don't want
Either of us to visit again
So, I hope to God
He's busy at the bakery.

The Final Nine

As I count down the days
Until I leave my place of employment
I cannot help but reminisce
About my tenure with the company.

I think back to those September days
When I was first trained to be on the road
An eager, bright eyed courier
Ready to take on the city.

Things and times changed
In the months that followed
New responsibilities were added on
To my life with the organization.

As the weeks drew on
The business expanded
And, expectations were put on me
That I was not ready to cope with.

Now, I am on the edge
Of this 22-month journey
Where one chapter of my life will end
A new one is about to begin.

Gone Too Soon

He came into our lives
As an elderly member last fall
But, we both loved him dearly
And, we were proud to call him our 'son'.

I was able to see him
Whenever my gal and I Skyped
His tongue hanging out of his mouth
He was so adorable.

Alas, he had his health problems
We were told his kidneys were weak
His stomach would swell with fluid
And, we had to get him drained occasionally.

We felt the pain he endured
As his body grew weaker
Praying that he would hold on
For a few days longer.

When the time came
We led him to the Rainbow Bridge
Fare thee well, dearest Duffy
Your mommy and daddy will always love you.

Giving (Port) Credit

In my time as a courier
I have travelled to various parts of the city
And, in some instances
I have gone beyond the borders of it.

However, today I was sent on a run
To a community I had never been to before
I had been through it on the Go Train
But, never got up close and personal to it.

The place sits just east of the mouth
Of the main river that flows
Through the city of Mississauga
A little hamlet in southern Peel Region.

I was transfixed
With the charm of the community
As shops lined the street
Known simply as Lakeshore.

I vowed to return here
Before I leave
So, I could soak up the atmosphere
Of this place known as Port Credit.

Early Arrivals

I received an email
About a week ago
Detailing about three envelopes I would receive
Each their own colour.

I was instructed
To open the envelopes in order
One for each day
During the first week of August.

Orange was to be opened first
On the day of my birth.
Turquoise the day after
For reasons that were unclear to me.

Finally, the last was to be white
To be unsealed on a momentous day
For it will be our anniversary
Two years since we've been together.

The only problem is
The envelopes arrived a fortnight early
I'm fighting the temptation
Not to follow my given orders.

Annual Pilgrimage

Every year during the summer
My fiancee and a few of her friends
Gather at a resort in Iowa
For their annual reunion.

This is for a family
Of a different sort
As they are all united
Over their love of dogs.

It is their annual fundraiser
Where the charity is
To help rescue these animals
From their former neglectful homes.

The pets are taken care of
And later, put up for adoption
So, they may find a home
With new loving parents.

I plan on joining this motley crew
For their celebration next year.
But, for now
I'm missing my baby.

Hard Work Proponents

There has been the odd gripe
Made my a colleague of mine
Who believes there are certain people
That are not pulling their weight in the office.

They believe in cutting corners
Or, coming up with new ideas
But, for those of us who cannot adapt
We struggle with the change.

There have also been rumblings
Of people saying things behind others' backs
All I see is the political spin
Going on within the workplace.

I try my best not to buy into the rhetoric
And, do the best job I can
Trying to keep my nose clean
In the process.

I believe in working hard
Not buying into the B.S.
Earning my paycheque
While counting down my days left.

It's A New Royalty

Recently, my online book retailer
Changed the way people were getting paid
Based on a certain segment
Of their online 'sales'.

Previously, the writers were compensated
For the amount of 'borrows'
A title was downloaded
Onto a customer's device.

Now, they are getting their royalties
Doled out depending upon
The number of pages
The lender has read of the title.

Authors were up in arms
Citing this was fractioning the pie
Into microscopic bits
Unfit for their consumption.

Personally, I think
It is an interesting new prospect
But, my opinion might change
When I read my royalty report.

Back To The Beginning

It only took me three weeks
But, I was able to catch a break from work
And now, I'm hanging with my friends
At our Starbucks hangout.

There are a few people
Hanging out here in the locale
A couple are working
While the rest are socializing.

This will change when
More people show up
However, I highly doubt
The work ethic will differ.

I admit I have missed
The atmosphere of my friends chatting
About various random topics
Of the day's events.

It is something I will be going without
When November rolls around
Because I will be part of a new group of writers
In my future Florida home.

Pan Am Chatter

Most of the talk so far tonight
Has been about the current Games
Discussing about various topics
Between the events and traffic.

The conversation has been spirited
Talking about the planning for them
Everything from transit to infrastructure
It has been quite compelling.

The chatter deviates towards
The probablity of Toronto
Hosting an Olympics
In the near future.

It was pointed out by one person
That the majority of the venues
Were built on a small basis
To make sure the events would sell out.

The Pan Ams have run smoothly, so far
However, I think an Olympics here
Would be more of a nightmare
And one, I'm hoping to avoid.

Cause of My Ailing Back

As I sit here in the Starbucks
I notice my back is starting to flair up again
I try to stretch it while sitting
In my chair at the main table.

I have speculated as to why
It acts up every now and again
Everything from a pelvic misalignment
To a pulled muscle.

However, one thing I seem to have noticed
When it does cause me discomfort
Is it usually aggravates
When I feel stressed.

With my writing project deadline looming
And, my final week of work upcoming
I feel myself getting tense
From the pressure I've put on myself.

I hope things will be easier
Once July is over
But, with my visa application upcoming
Relief might be delayed longer.

NaNo Planning

The Municipal Liaison for
The Toronto region of NaNoWriMo
Is having an open discussion
About possible events this November.

We are discussing various
Social activities to occur
During the month
Along with our different write-ins.

Some are very popular
And, we intend to keep them in our rotation
Others with lower turnouts
We are thinking of scrapping.

I have to admit I am envious
Of all of the fun things that are being planned
For there is no guarantee I will
Be here come the eleventh month.

I hope there will be
A good group where I am moving to
But, there will never be replacing
My colleagues in TONaNo.

Free Smut

I decided to try something
With the release of my short story
It will hurt me in my pocketbook
But, it is a way to get my work out there.

I am offering it for free
For a few days
In hopes it will generate some interest
Among the reading public.

At my last check
It has been downloaded seventeen times
Twelve from patrons in the States
Five more from those in the U.K.

I would love for it
To go to readers in more countries
However, I am happy with
The fact it's being picked up at all.

I have to confess
I am worried about who will read it
Because the subject matter
Is not suitable for all audiences.

Before I Leave Canada

As someone who has called this land
His home for the majority of his life
There are many things I will miss
When I leave the only home I have known.

I will miss the iconic chain
Of coffee and bake shops
That has provided me addictive sustenance
For years of enjoyment.

I will miss my writing friends
As few as I have
They have been supportive of me
As I have of them and their endeavours.

I will miss my family
Even though I admit I am not close to them
But, they are the only ones I have
Their absence will leave a hole within my life.

Finally, I will miss this country
The great place known as Canada
I hope to return one day
With my new family in tow.

www.ingramcontent.com/pod-product-compliance
Lightning Source LLC
Chambersburg PA
CBHW070523030426
42337CB00016B/2084